Fingerpower® Transposer

Primer Level

Melodic Technic Exercises with Integrated Tra

T0056023

by Wesley Schaum

Foreword

This unique series integrates the benefits of Fingerpower® exercises with basic transposing. Transposing helps develop ear training and awareness of melodic contour. At the Primer Level, the student uses C, F and G hand positions in both treble and bass staffs.

These exercises present simple melodic and harmonic intervals. The student learns to recognize these intervals on the printed page, hear the different sounds, and also experience the feeling in the hand as various intervals are played.

Each exercise has melodic elements delineated by phrase marks. Students are taught to recognize phrase groups that recur in the same piece. This process helps in learning and memorizing these exercises. Awareness of phrase groups also helps to enhance music reading skills beyond this book.

EXCLUSIVELY DISTRIBUTED BY

HAL•LEONARD® CORPORATION

7777 W. BLUEMOUND RD. P.O. BOX 13819 MILWAUKEE, WI 53213

ISBN-13: 978-1-62906-020-0

1. 2/4 Pattern – C Position

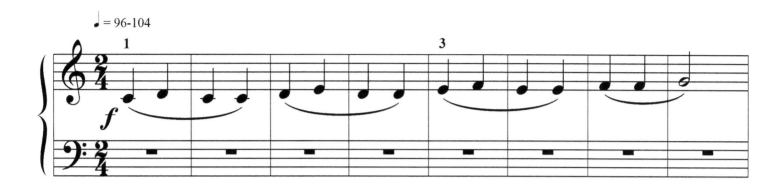

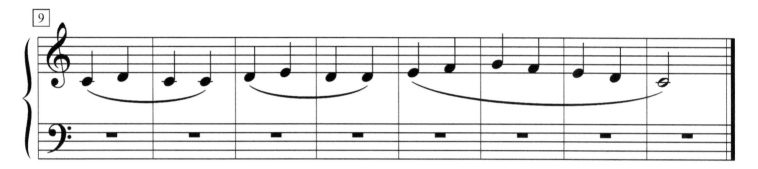

Transposed to G Position:

Teacher's Note: Phrase marks are intended to show groups of notes that form patterns. Some of these patterns recur in each piece. The student should be taught how to recognize patterns which are the same. This makes the piece easier to learn and to memorize.

2. 3/4 Pattern – G Position

Transposed to C Position:

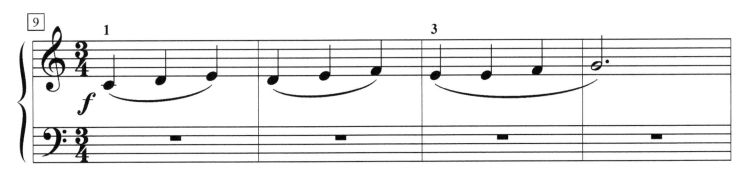

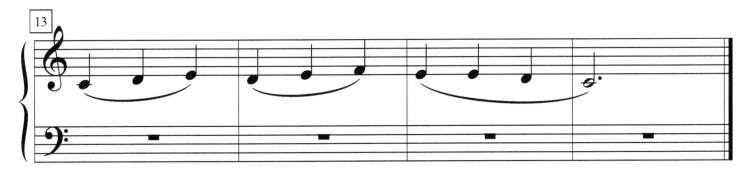

3. 4/4 Pattern – C Position

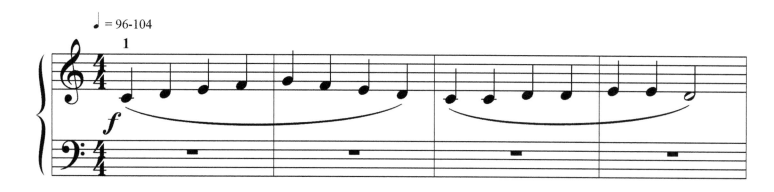

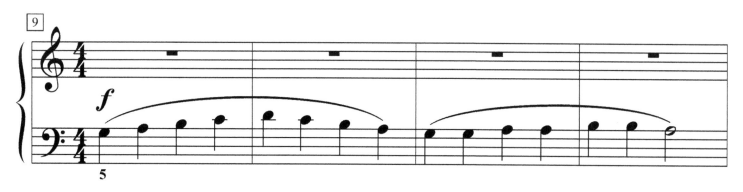

Transposed to G Position:

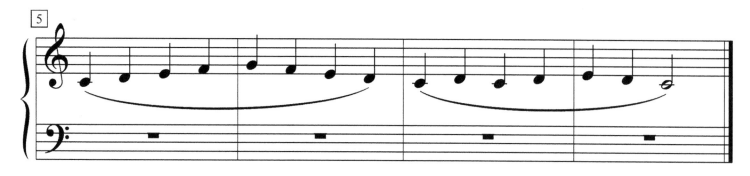

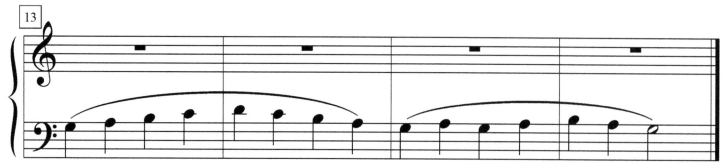

4. Pattern with 3rds – C Position

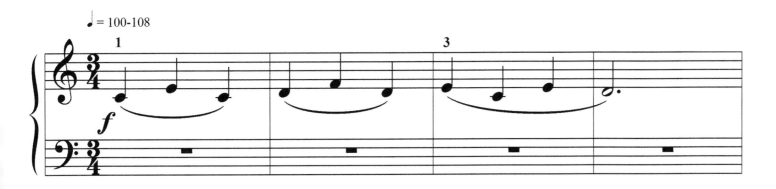

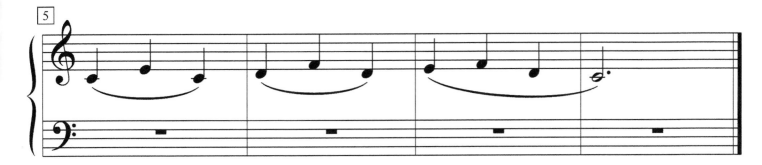

Transposed to G Position:

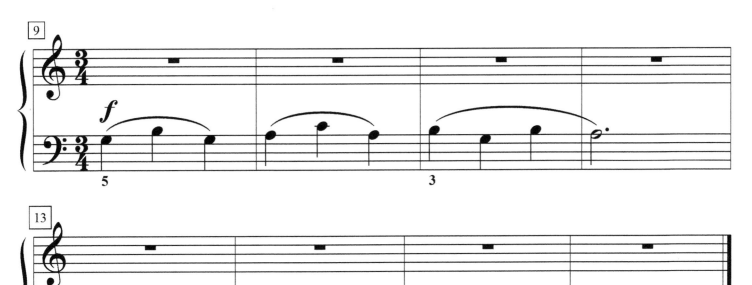

Teacher's Note: Point out the intervals of a 3rd, up and down, that occur in measures with quarter notes. Be sure the student understands that the curved lines are all <u>slurs</u>, NOT ties.

5. Five-Finger Pattern with 3rds – G Position

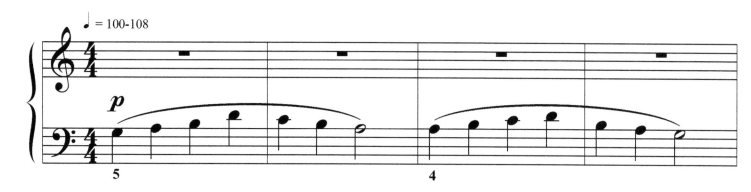

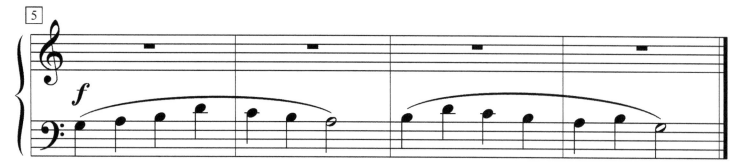

Transposed to C Position:

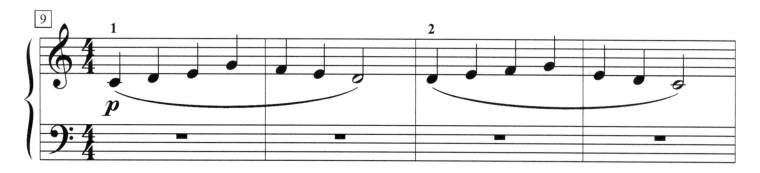

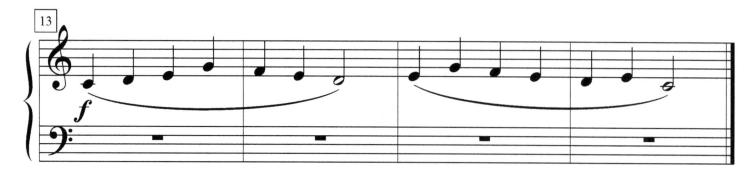

6. Broken and Blocked 3rds – C Position

Transposed to G Position:

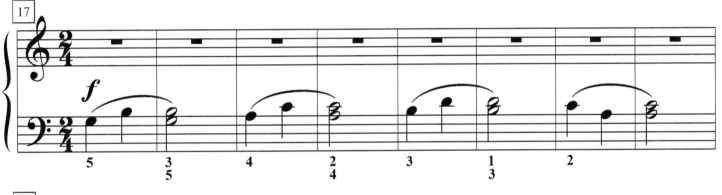

7. 4/4 Pattern in F Position

Transposed to C Position:

Teacher's Note: The F Position is introduced with the B-flat as an accidental. The key signature for F major will be introduced later.

8. 3/4 Pattern in C Position

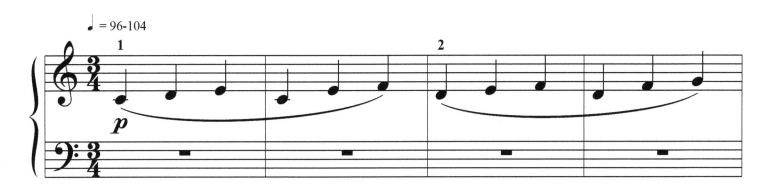

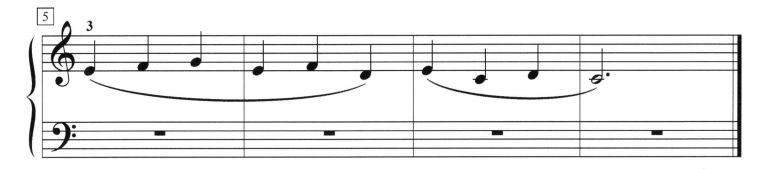

Transposed to F Position:

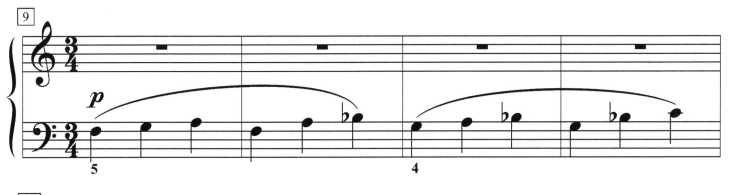

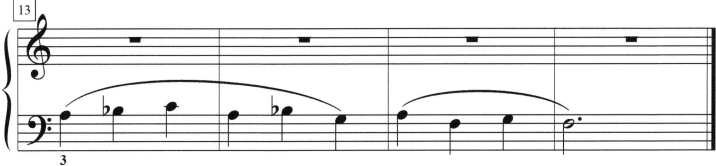

9. Right Hand C Position Pattern

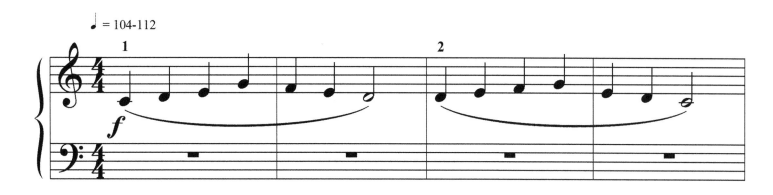

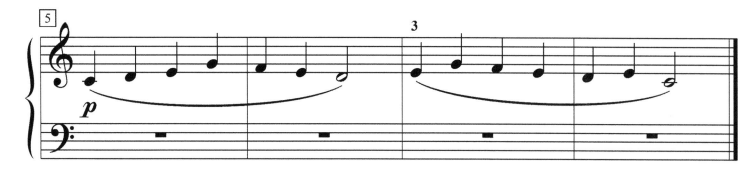

Left Hand C Position:

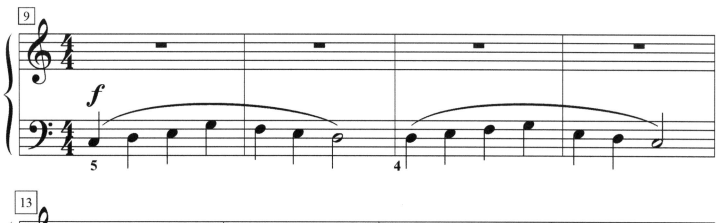

Teacher's Note: Point out that the Left Hand C Position is **one octave lower** than the Right Hand C Position.

For the purposes of this book, *playing one octave lower or higher is considered a form of transposition.* This may differ from a stricter definition of the term.

10. Left Hand C Position Pattern

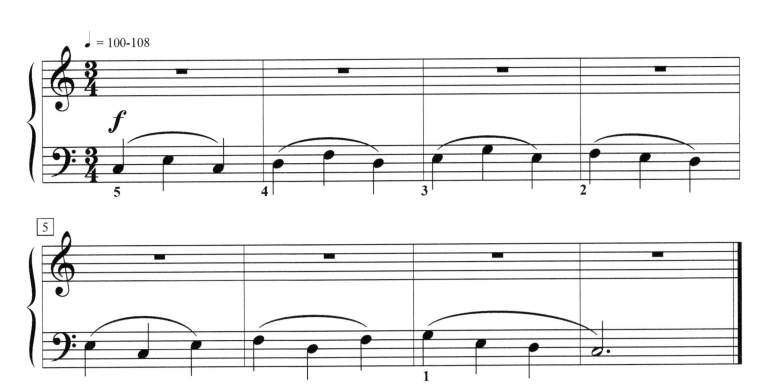

Right Hand C Position:

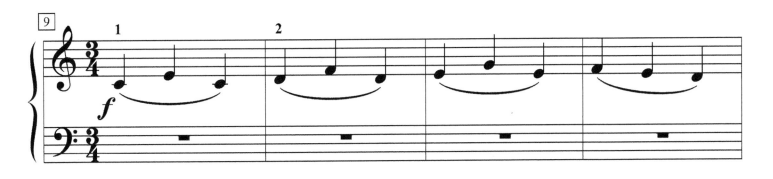

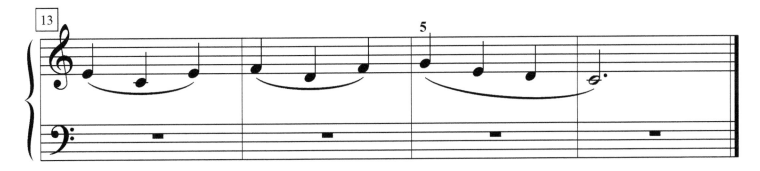

11. Pattern with 3rds and 4ths – F Position

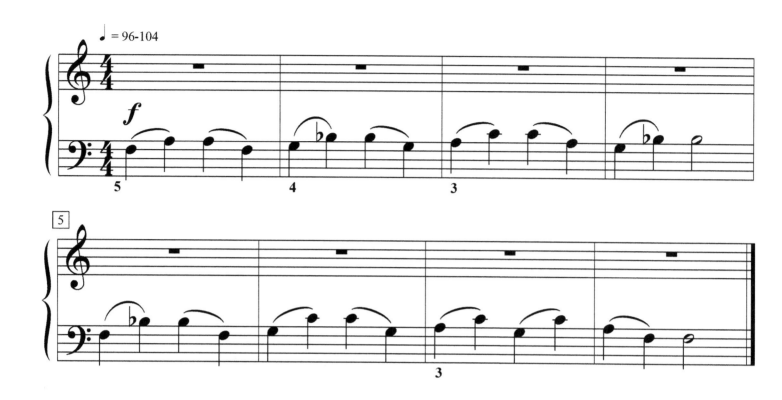

Transposed to Right Hand C Position:

Teacher's Note: Point out the various intervals of a 3rd and 4th, up and down, as indicated by the slurs.

12. Left Hand G Position Pattern

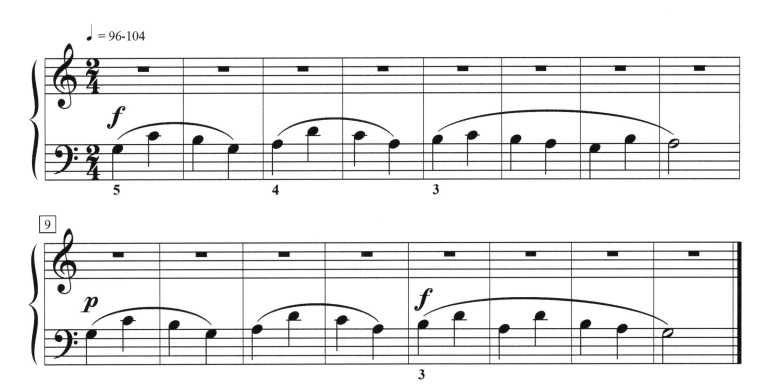

Right Hand G Position:

Teacher's Note: Point out that the Right Hand G Position is one octave higher than the Left Hand G Position. Also show the student where intervals of 3rds and 4ths occur.

13. Right Hand G Position Pattern

♩ = 104-112

Left Hand G Position:

Teacher's Note: Ask the student to find phrases that have the same groups of notes.

14. Pattern with 4ths and 5ths – C Position

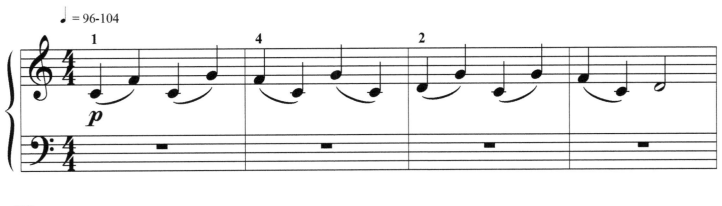

Transposed to G Position:

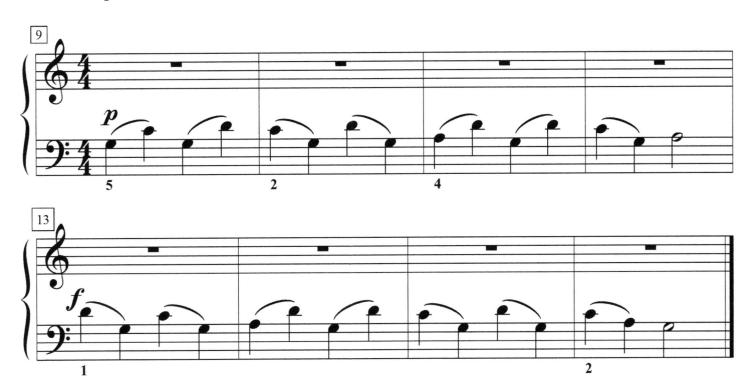

Teacher's Note: Point out the intervals of 4ths and 5ths, up and down, as indicated by slurs.

15. 3rds, 4ths and 5ths – G Position

Transposed to C Position:

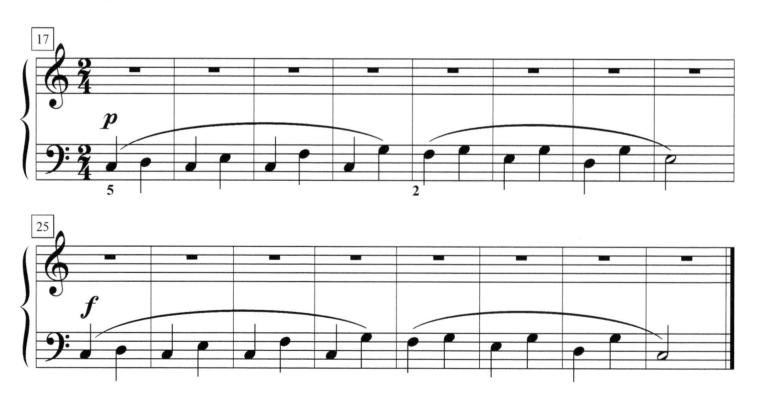

16. Pattern for Right Hand F Position

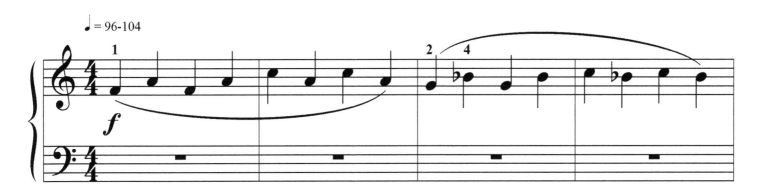

Left Hand F Position:

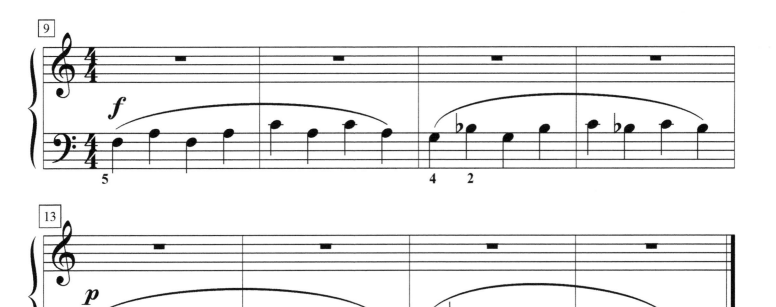

17. Pattern with 8th Notes – G Position

Transposed to F Position:

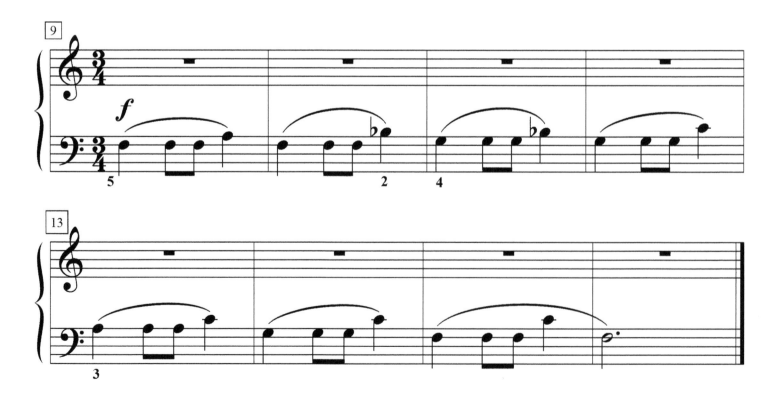

18. Alternating Hands – C Position

Transposed to G Position:

19. Alternating Hands with Staccato – C Position

Transposed to G Position:

20. Melody and Accompaniment – C Position

Transposed to F Position:

21. 8th Notes with Staccato – C Position

Right Hand C Position:

Transposed to Left Hand G Position:

Transposed to Right Hand F Position: